Stop Eating

The Proven Steps to Take Control, Stop Emotional Eating, and Live Your Best Life

Table Of Contents

Introduction

I want to thank you for purchasing this book, Stop Eating - The Proven Steps to Take Control, Stop Emotional Eating, and Live Your Best Life.

Do you find yourself always looking for a bag of chips or reaching for the ice-cream tub when you're upset or even just bored? It might start out with a little bit of unhealthy junk food when you have cravings, but ultimately you end up being a binge eater elbow deep in food.

At some point, most people tend to develop an unhealthy relationship with food. I've been there, and I know how hard it can be to take control and stop even when you realize you need to. Every time you're worried or anxious about something, you probably head straight for the fridge to drown your sorrows in food.

Occasionally indulging in some comfort food when you feel down is completely okay, but for some of us, it starts from there and ends up an impulsive habit that you can't seem to take control of. If you are reading this, however, you have taken the first step to make a change and stop this self-destructive behavior.

Emotional eating can be very unhealthy and lead to excessive weight gain with other related conditions. It might make you feel good at first, but at the end of the day, it won't solve your problems, and you'll still go to bed feeling upset. Instead of adding to your problems, begin taking control of things one at a time and stop eating!

Chapter 1: What Is Emotional Eating?

If we are completely honest, we've all been there. It could be a bag of chips while watching TV, stuffing our face with junk food while studying for a big test, eating right out of the ice-cream tub when something upsets us, and the list goes on. Most people do these things without even thinking about it. This is because people often use food to deal with feelings. Emotional eating is when you eat as a way to relieve negative emotions and not when you are hungry. It's used as a coping strategy and can end up causing more problems in the future. Over time, this kind of unhealthy eating can also lead to many eating disorders like bulimia. It's surprising when you realize just how many people tend to deal with problematic situations using comfort food and how other people actually enable this tendency. Have you noticed how your friends always offer to buy you some ice cream when they see you're feeling down? It might seem nice at the time, but it just fuels the bad habit. Eating a lot of food when life gets tough will never be a solution. It will make you feel better for a few minutes, but in the long run, you're just adding more problems like weight gain to the list.

Emotional eating needs to be given serious consideration and warrants consultation with a doctor. It has in common with eating disorders, so it's important that you take notice of the signs of emotional eating as early as possible and take control. Instead of reaching for food to deal with negative emotions, it is essential to learn how you can more effectively deal with tough situations. Your coping strategies need to be healthy and something you will benefit from. Emotional eating will give you a temporary respite, but at the end of the day it will not solve the problem but lead to more.

Binge eating, or compulsive eating, is an aggravated form of emotional eating. You don't realize it when you reach for your comfort food once in a while, and over time it can develop into a serious problem that will be much harder to deal with.

A lot of research has been done to gather statistical data about binge eating disorders. Based on information from the UK, the US and Europe, the NEDA[1] were able to see how commonly prevalent it is. According to these studies, in 2007, when around 9,000 people were asked about any eating disorders, 2% of men and 3.5% of women said they had suffered from it at some point in their life. This proved that binge eating issues were much more common than anorexia or bulimia cases. In fact, it is even more common than cases of HIV or even breast cancer. When a study was done on 496 girls of an adolescent age, it was found that 5.2% of them suffered from eating disorder symptoms before they even reached 20. And these were just related to a few identified disorders. Binge eating disorder usually begins around the late teens when people, especially women, are subjected to more opinions on their appearance. The rest of the 40% are males who also suffer from this issue. Out of all those people who face binge eating disorders, less than half of them will seek treatment for it. At least 3 people from 10, who enroll in weight loss programs, have suffered from binge eating disorders. It is important to identify and deal with the problem before it escalates.

Initially, a little food might satisfy you, but your problem is still there, and you end up eating more to try and feel better. It's an indirect way of feeding your emotions. Emotional eaters

---

[1] ("National Eating Disorders Association", 2018)

transition from a little bit of eating to massive binges to deal with the lack of salvation from the initial eating. This kind of compulsive eating is often related to low self-esteem and body image issues. There are a lot of people around you who are dealing with the same problem, so don't think you're alone. The first step is identifying the problem. Once you've identified it, you need to find the root of it. What led you to emotional eating?

Signs of Emotional Eating

There are many warning signs in your behavior that indicate emotional eating problems. Some of the signs of emotional eating are craving junk foods all the time, feeling suddenly and intensely hungry, and having the urge to eat when something bothers you. Read on and see if any of them resonate with you.

- You tend to keep some food handy when you need to study for a big test or have a lot of work to catch up on. You unconsciously keep eating as you work. This can be in the middle of the day or late at night as well.

- You eat whenever you feel sad or anxious or angry or even bored. It becomes a subconscious habit where you always reach for food in response to negative emotions that you don't know how to deal with. Your automatic response is always to reach out for food.

- You buy a lot of comfort food like chocolate and cake and ice cream when you feel down. Most comfort foods are junk food with no nutritional value, and you know this, but these are what make you feel better.

- You keep eating even when you are trying to lose

weight. You know you're overweight and need to control your eating, but you can't seem to stop yourself from reaching for food. Even though you may be worried about your weight, you still end up eating.

- You eat even when you're not hungry and know that you shouldn't eat. Your eating is out of your control, and you can't stop even when you know you should. Your cravings seem to take control over you, and you go out of your way to satisfy them.

- Eating makes you feel good and positive, and you start to depend on food to make you feel happy. Dependence on food is very different from an appreciation of food. This unhealthy dependence makes you think that only food can make you feel better. You associate happiness with food. You need to eat even when you're happy because you think of it as a way to celebrate.

- You think about food all the time. Even when you're not eating or just ate, you think about what to eat again. You are fascinated with food and love eating.

- You talk about food with words like love, tempting, decadent, and sinful. These are emotion-related words, and you associate them with food.

- You never feel satisfied no matter how much you eat. Even when you know you ate enough and feel full, you can't stop yourself from eating more. You might have just finished a meal, but you feel dissatisfied within moments and end up eating again. You obsess over food. After you finish a meal, you're immediately thinking about what to eat later.

- You have untimely cravings all the time. You get the

urge to eat something out of the blue and have no explanation for it. Your cravings are not related to hunger and can hit you at any time. If you don't satisfy your craving, you feel restless and anxious about it all day.

A lot of people might tell you that it's perfectly normal to eat whenever you want. They might encourage you to go ahead and eat if it makes you feel better. They may come to you with a lot of chocolate or some kind of treat to console you after a breakup or whenever you're upset, telling you that you have the right to drown your sorrows in food after all that you've gone through. This, however, is the worst way to tackle a situation and can cause a lot of damage in the long term. Eating to feel better once or twice is okay, but if you are emotionally dependent on food every time you face a problem, the eating has become another problem. Emotional eating should not be your long-term solution for dealing with issues. You need to find a more sustainable and healthy way to do so.

Factors Affecting Emotional Eating

Negative Affectivity

Negative affectivity is a trait in your personality that is related to negative emotions and low self-esteem. Some people have high levels of this trait, and it has been shown to predict emotional eating in them. Many studies show that people indulge in emotional eating only when they undergo negative emotions. Instead of articulating how they are feeling, they engage in binge eating. This type of behavior is an inability to regulate the negative affect trait; however, it's not just this trait that causes emotional eating. If the person has trouble emotionally coping with issues coupled with a habit of avoiding problems, then it can lead to emotional eating. Negative affect along with other variables can spur emotional eating in a person.

Childhood Development

Emotional eating develops in the early years for some people. Some parents tend to give children their favorite food to make them feel better if they are upset. Over time, this makes the child associate emotions with food. When parents enable this kind of behavior, the child does not realize that what they are doing is wrong. As they grow up, they start to reach for food to make themselves feel better if they failed a test or had a bad day. The kind of emotional eating that develops early can be very challenging to deal with because it has deep roots. Old habits are the hardest to break.

Eating Disorders

Emotional eating is deeply related to many eating disorders like bulimia. This type of eating may be a precursor for such conditions because they have similar characteristics. Emotional eating can also develop as a result of eating disorders. For instance, people who suffer from bulimia nervosa tend to eat emotionally and binge before they force themselves to vomit. It is ideal to identify it in the beginning and gain control before it leads to more serious conditions. Emotional eating and other eating disorders have characteristics such as maladaptive coping, aversion to negative feelings, and coping through food in one capacity or another. Emotional eating is a very common trait in those who are leading up to or already suffering from some serious eating disorders that need medical attention.

Biological Factors

The body itself affects your food intake and preferences. When you're stressed, your body pushes you to eat more fatty or sugary food. The reason for this is high insulin levels, high ghrelin levels, and high cortisol levels in the body. Ghrelin is a hunger hormone that plays a role in all this. Secretion of the cortisol hormone increases in response to stress in the body. It then triggers a stress response that leads to a faster rate of heartbeat and breathing, increased blood flow, and visual acuity. Another part of this stress response is increased appetite in order to gain energy from food for this fight-or-flight response. People who suffer from chronic stress have a lot of cortisol secretion in their body and thus tend to develop emotional eating due to it.

Studies have shown that foods high in fat and sugar tend to have a dampening effect on stress. This is why these foods become comfort food over time as you use them to feel better when you're stressed out. This biological factor is responsible for you getting those comfort food cravings when you experience stress or negative emotions; however, the levels can vary between people. Some people have adrenal glands that secrete more glucocorticoids than others when there is stress. These people have a greater tendency toward hyperplasia, which is often a catalyst for binge eating. It is also seen to be common in those whose bodies take more time to get rid of the glucocorticoids in their bloodstream. Thus these biological factors affect emotional eating tendencies in many people. The more stress they deal with, the more the pattern of emotional eating develops in them.

External Factors

The food industry has had a huge impact on our relationship with food. All the marketing and advertisements imply that we will be happy when we have food in our hands. There are huge billboards all around us of happy people laughing and eating junk food, so it's natural that we want to enact the same image. Food is associated with celebrations. Every time there is a wedding, party, or festival, people talk about food and gather for a meal.

Chapter 2: Difference between Emotional and Physical Hunger

You need to learn to differentiate between emotional hunger and physical hunger. Emotional hunger can often be so powerful that you easily mistake it for actual physical hunger. You have to become more conscious about identifying it and not indulging in emotional hunger.

- Physical hunger usually comes on slowly and is not so noticeable unless you haven't eaten for quite some time. You don't feel the need to urgently eat when you are physically hungry but just become aware that your body needs food.

- Emotional hunger has a very sudden onset and works like a craving. You feel an urgent need to satisfy it. It's not related to the body actually needing food.

- Physical hunger can be satisfied with any form of food. Your body will be satiated with anything from vegetables to meat.

- Emotional hunger is sated only with specific kinds of food. These are the comfort foods we reach for when we feel down. Only junk food that gives you a rush—usually in the form of sugary food or junk like pizza—will satisfy emotional hunger.

- When you eat from physical hunger, you are more aware of the food. Your stomach will feel satisfied once you eat enough.

- Emotional eating is quite mindless, and you just keep eating without being conscious of it. You don't feel satiated for a long time, and you stop only when you have filled yourself with food from your stomach up to your throat.

- Physical hunger is felt from your belly. Your stomach growls or hurts if you haven't eaten for too long. This subsides once you eat a meal.

- Emotional hunger is not related to the stomach but to the mind. This hunger arises in the form of thoughts and cravings where your focus is on your comfort foods.

- When your body is physically hungry, you feel good and satisfied after a proper meal. You don't think about it later.

Emotional hunger gives you momentary satisfaction when you indulge it, but later you feel guilty and ashamed. This is because you know that you didn't eat because your body needed it and that it's actually bad for you to eat that way.

All of these are some basic ways to differentiate between when you are physically hungry and when you are emotionally hungry. Your body only needs food when you are physically hungry. Overindulging in emotional hunger can be detrimental to your physical and mental health. Start to be more conscious of identifying what type of hunger you experience and eating only when you need to. Physical hunger will be satisfied with some food. Food will satisfy emotional hunger temporarily, but the feelings and problems will still remain and make you feel worse later.

Chapter 3: Impact of Emotional Eating

Now let's take a look at some of the impact that emotional eating can have on your life. It might feel perfectly natural to reach for comfort food in certain situations, but you will think twice the next time when you realize how it affects you in the long term.

- When you eat emotionally, you don't pay attention to the reason for your negative emotions. You get so preoccupied with the idea of food and just start eating instead of thinking about what triggered those emotions.

- You end up ignoring the issue that set off those negative emotions. The emotional eating will help you push the problem away but just for a few moments. When the eating is said and done, the problem is still there. Even if you suppress it and don't allow yourself to think about it, it's still present in the back of your mind and in your life. Closing your eyes to it will not make it go away. Emotional eating can temporarily dispel the feelings, but it will not solve the underlying problem.

- An endless loop is created where the same feelings keep arising and you keep suppressing them with food. This is because you did not deal with the actual problem at hand. It's also because you keep using the same method to push away your problems. Because eating doesn't solve the problem, you will just recreate the same situation again and again. Every time a problem arises, you will get stressed about it. Then you'll eat to deal with that stress and feel good for a while. In the meantime, you ignore and momentarily forget the problem that stressed you out, but it remains unresolved and comes up again. Each time the same stress recurs, you eat to deal with it. This same cycle goes on and on in an unending loop until you really deal with the problem and solve it without emotional eating.

- Reaching out for comfort food too many times will just make you emotionally dependent on it in the long run. You will rely on food to dispel any negative emotions you don't want to deal with. You will depend on food to feel happy. Every time you feel down, you will crave certain foods to deal with your emotions. Being denied food and not being able to satisfy your cravings will make you irritable and antsy. In a way, emotional eating can become similar to drug addiction.

- Your state of life is an illusion. You think you're fine and happy, but you really aren't. Emotional eating did not solve any of the problems in your life, and they continue to persist. Food is meant to provide your body with nutrition and energy. It is not the solution to anything other than physical hunger. Eating emotionally will make you feel good for that moment because of the secretion of serotonin and because your mind links happiness to food. You have conditioned your body to feel good only when you're eating. This state of happiness is nothing but a temporary illusion. Keeping yourself happy with food allows the problem to plague you for a long time, and it will keep triggering the negative emotions that you're trying to suppress. You can be truly happy if you learn to deal with the problem and those negative emotions in the right way.

- Your body has been abused by all the unnecessary eating. It is built to process and store only a certain amount of food. Emotional eating causes you to eat a lot more than you need and a lot more than your body can possibly get used to. You gain extra weight, and your digestive system has to work extra hard to process the amount of food you're taking in. All the extra food makes you tired, and your body gets exhausted with all the extra work it's doing. Just because you exercise right after you binge-eat does not mean it's okay. You're just straining your body even more. Even if you look healthy and have the ideal body weight, emotional eating and all the extra exercising is very draining on your system. It can cause many problems with your organs and your body. Problems like high cholesterol are very commonly associated with this kind of eating. Your body will work and last according to how you treat it.

- One of the most obvious impacts of emotional eating is weight gain. If you keep turning to food to deal with problems, it's just a matter of time before it will show in your body. It will start with a little weight gain, but it can slowly lead to becoming overweight or obese. There are some emotional eaters who combat the extra weight by exercising a lot—and this is still a problem even if they're not overweight—but the majority of emotional eaters are heavier than their average counterparts. This weight gain can have negative effects on your mind as well as your body. Weight gain causes issues like obesity and has many health implications.

- Weight gain due to emotional eating does not affect only your physical health. It has a huge impact on your mental well-being as well. Your changing body stresses you out, and your self-esteem suffers when you compare yourself to society's standards of beauty. This just leads to more binge eating to feel better. The stress about body image can even cause you to channel the negativity toward yourself and make you hate yourself. This kind of stress can cause eating disorders like anorexia and bulimia.

Chapter 4: The Cycle of Emotional Eating

Many times you will notice that food cravings are at their strongest when you're emotionally weak. When you're stressed, bored, or facing some difficult problem, you tend to turn toward food as a source of comfort. This emotional dependency can sabotage your efforts to lose weight and also prevent you from actually solving the real issue at hand. Emotional eating is a maladaptive way to cope with negative emotions like stress, boredom, and fear. Many events in your daily life—conflicts in your relationships, excessive workload, financial problems, health issues—can easily trigger this unhealthy craving for food. There are some people for whom such issues curb their appetite so that they lose a lot of weight, but others turn toward food to deal with emotional distress.

Over time, your emotions become tightly tied up with your food. Every time you feel sad or angry, you automatically reach for comfort food to make yourself feel better. This food just serves as a distraction and does not solve any problems. Instead of dealing with painful situations, we turn our focus to the food and avoid dealing with what is actually important. When someone we know goes through a breakup, we might encourage them to go ahead and eat that tub of ice cream, even though we know it's completely unhealthy. The same thing is repeated over and over again—every time something upsetting happens, you turn toward food.

Regardless of the trigger, the end result of overeating will always be the same. You are harming your body, gaining extra weight, and not solving your real problems. In fact, the guilt of this emotional overeating just adds to the burden. All this leads to an unhealthy cycle of a trigger making you eat too much, feeling guilty over it, and feeling bad again. The negative emotions are temporarily suppressed, but they arise again. It is important to break out of this cycle and get back on track.

Here's how you can start keeping track of your eating habits:

- Maintain a food diary. Write down what time you eat, what food you eat, how much you eat. Also, write down how you were feeling when you ate and how hungry you were at the time. This will help you establish a pattern over time.

- Start paying attention to and differentiating between physical and emotional hunger. If you just had lunch or dinner, your cravings are not from physical hunger. Drink some water and focus on something else when you get such cravings.

- Start practicing ways to deal with your stress in a healthy way. Many people recommend yoga or meditation as an effective way to manage stress.

- Reach out for support in your journey. Find people to share your feelings with who will support and encourage you through it.

- Don't allow yourself to get bored. Find a way to occupy yourself when you have nothing to do. Don't lie in front of the TV and reach for a ton of junk food. Take a walk or play with your pets to occupy yourself if there is nothing to do. Mindless snacking can develop into a very unhealthy habit.

- Get rid of all the excess junk food in your house. Having

it around will just tempt you to reach out for it every time something triggers your emotional eating habit. You are less likely to indulge in it if you have to make a trip to the grocery store for it. By the time you get there, your craving will probably have subsided.

- Just because you are starting a healthier diet does not mean you have to deprive yourself of all the food you like. Most fad diets fail because they deprive you of all the food you like to eat. Eat more healthy foods but allow yourself to enjoy some occasional treats. Don't stick to the same treat but instead add some variety so that you don't start making associations with that food again.

- Start snacking in a healthier way. Mindless snacking is one of the fastest ways to gain extra weight. Keep some healthier snack options available so that if you suddenly feel hungry, you have something to munch on. Keep some cut fruit in the fridge or have a handful of nuts. These are much better options than eating a whole box of cookies or a bag of chips.

- Forgive yourself for any setbacks. Just because you could not control yourself that one time does not mean you can't the next day. Think about what made you fall off the wagon and try to deal with it better the next time. One bad day does not make everything fail for you. Just stay focused and keep trying to reduce the number of bad days. You can only improve if you learn from your bad experiences. Don't give up and fall back on binge eating to deal with the stress. This will only make all your efforts futile.

All these are small and simple steps you can take to deal with your emotional eating. If these fail, you can try a more intensive method or consult professionals for guidance and treatment. There is more on this later.

Chapter 5: How to Stop Emotional Eating

If you want to gain control over your life and stop emotional eating, you need to understand a few basic things. Firstly, it cannot be done in a single day just because you suddenly say you will stop eating that way. The problem is deep-rooted and will require some effort, but it's not impossible. Don't think of it as something too easy or too difficult. The first step is to identify the problem and then you can start dealing with it. It won't be a single step toward a healthier you but an entire process that this book will help you with. As you go step by step, you will slowly be able to stop eating unless you are truly hungry, and you will learn how to deal with your emotions in a healthier way.

Diagnosis of Emotional Eating

Many different health care providers or specialists help to evaluate and treat emotional eating. Over the years it has become a much more prevalent problem than it was a couple of decades ago. Emotional eating is a major contributing factor to obesity and excessive weight gain in people, and this has made professionals more aware of the need to deal with the problem. When you know that the problem is serious, it is best to consult a professional for help. You might need a consultation with a psychologist, help from a pediatrician, or monitoring of your eating. Sometimes just one doctor is enough to help you out, but for those who deal with a more severe problem like an associated eating disorder, multiple sources might be required.

The initial diagnosis of emotional eating is made after a proper physical examination and tests to check for any medical conditions or genetic factors. There are some standardized tests with questions for the patient to answer in order to assess the condition. The patient's mental health history is studied to check for eating disorders like pica or bulimia or any mental illnesses. All this together is used to determine whether the person suffers from emotional eating and the extent of it.

Identifying the Triggers of Emotional Eating

You need to start by identifying what triggers you to start eating when you're not even hungry. Think about the last few times you had sudden cravings or binged on food. Write these instances down on a list. Seeing it written down can be quite revealing and help you see the pattern of ignoring problems and eating to combat them. There can be many different reasons for emotional eating. To deal with your emotional eating, you must identify what triggers it. What kinds of situations, people, or feelings make you want to eat your comfort foods? Do you eat when you feel sad to drown your sorrows? Or do you eat when you want to celebrate an event? Does being around a particular person make you want to indulge in food to feel better? Everyone has different triggers, so don't shrug off a reason just because it seems normal to you. Some people are triggered when they are stress about work. You might be emotionally eating when you have to do something you didn't want to. You might compulsively eat every time you see food or pass by a food stall. Maybe you eat every time you think of or hear about a particular food, or you feel obligated to eat just because you know it's lunch or dinnertime and can't seem to skip it even if you're not hungry. You might just keep eating whenever you're bored and have nothing to do. Some people eat more when they are stressed by the people around them, like relatives at a family gathering. All of these and many more could be triggers for your unhealthy emotional eating habits. Until you identify them, you cannot start to overcome the habit.

Ideally, everyone would eat only when they were hungry and only as much as their body really needed. We would all be able to stop eating as soon as our stomach was full and not hungry anymore; however, most of us eat a lot when affected by extrinsic factors like being part of a celebration or when dealing with stress. This is why you need to work on building a healthy relationship with food. Your attitude should be one of "eat to live" rather than "live to eat." Appreciating food is very different from being obsessed with it. An unhealthy relationship with food can be the root of many problems, both physically and emotionally. Identifying the triggers for your eating will make you more conscious of your actions in the future. You will become more aware of what you are doing every time you reach for food. Once you know your triggers, you have a better chance of dealing with them.

Understanding Your Reasons

Once you have written down all the triggers that lead to your emotional eating, try to understand why they affect you negatively. It may have seemed completely normal to eat that way in some situations, but when you compare your behavior to others', you will see the issue. For instance, if you go to a birthday party, it might seem compulsory for you to eat the cake, but your friend might say no. At that time, you probably thought it weird for them to refuse cake since it's a basic part of the occasion, but now that you question it, you realize it's just a conditioned habit and that you don't really have to eat it if you don't want to. The problem is that you never stopped to think about it and just ate the cake because it was there.

Start looking at the list of your triggers and question why each one affects you. Write down the answers beside the list. Don't write answers like "it's normal," but instead think about what makes you want to indulge in emotional eating in the moment of that particular trigger. Keep questioning yourself till you realize how you linked that particular situation to eating over the years.

Detach These Triggers from Food

After all the self-questioning, you know most of the reasons behind why these triggers prompt you to eat. The next step is to work toward disassociating food from these triggers. Try to understand how each link was established. At some point in the past, you started eating in response to a particular situation, and over time your body became conditioned to it. You need to identify what that situation was and accept that this link you established is not really normal and is very different from how other people react to the same situation. If you want to stop yourself from continuing the same self-destructive behavior, you first have to accept that it is not healthy and is incongruent with how others deal with situations.

Once you start accepting that it was wrong to link eating with those triggers, you will start understanding that it was all in your mind. In reality, the triggers don't have any relation to eating, and you shouldn't link them in that way. The triggers have to be separated from the eating since the two things are completely different issues. Eating should be linked only to physical hunger that has to be satisfied to provide the body with energy. The triggers that cause emotional eating are completely irrelevant to why you should eat.

For instance, think about how you associate food with celebrations. You will see that most celebrations in the past have had a lot of food involved. Thanksgiving tables are always filled with food, and everyone eats till they're stuffed and not just till their hunger is sated. As kids, we went to fast food places like McDonald's right after exams were over to celebrate with sodas and burgers. As adults, we treat ourselves to a fancy restaurant dinner when the paychecks come in. Celebrations have always been deemed incomplete without a lot of food to enjoy them with. This is why our brains are synced to associate food with celebrations every single time, but you need to realize that it's a very illogical way of thinking. Why do you need to eat excessive food to celebrate something good? It's not just the fact that you eat unhealthy food but also how much more you eat than necessary.

When there is something to celebrate, embrace the feeling of happiness it gives you. Process the emotion itself and don't do it with food. All that food will just counteract your positive feelings and make you punish yourself later when you gain extra weight. Everyone is always complaining about the holiday weight they gain after the festivities are over, but no one stops to think about why they eat so much in the first place. You can still eat some good meals during the holidays, but you don't have to indulge to the point where all your clothes stop fitting you. When you start to consciously think about this, you will slowly stop eating compulsively every time something good happens. Don't distract yourself with food but embrace the happy emotions by themselves.

Another example is dealing with cravings. Sudden cravings for food are one of the most common symptoms of emotional eating. Most of the time, these cravings are associated with junk food or any unhealthy food that gives you a momentary rush. When you have such cravings, you might think that it's a form of hunger and you absolutely have to satisfy it, but you need to start thinking about these cravings more and realize that they are linked only to your mind and not your body.

If you stop and ask yourself why you keep craving a particular food, you will understand better. Most of the time it's because you associate that food with something good that happened and eating it makes you feel better again. There are certain foods like pancakes or waffles that your mom might have treated you with when you were younger. As you grow older, eating these things imparts a sense of comfort and goodness in you again, but if you think about it, you felt good because of your mother and not the food. The food was just one way she showed you love, but it was not the root of it. If you want to feel better in a situation, think about her and not the food.

Deal with the Triggers

Emotional eating usually happens when you don't want to deal with a certain emotion or situation. In order to turn off this trigger, you need to first deal with it. Eating cannot act as a makeshift solution. If you don't deal with the problem and try to resolve it, it won't go away. Eating will just suppress your emotions and help you push the problem to the back of your mind. You might feel better and not think of it for a while, but it will continue to come forward until you actually resolve it. Because emotional eating is largely associated with stress, one of the most crucial aspects of this is stress management. As you read on, stress management will be dealt with in a more thorough manner to help you through it.

Another thing you need to deal with is straying from your diet. Most people with excessive weight gain try to go on diets to get healthier and lose weight. The first issue arises when they choose unhealthy fad diets that do more harm than good to the body. These diets are designed to make you fail, but even when you do find a healthy diet, you might occasionally slip up. It's okay if you eat something outside the confines of your diet once in a while; you don't need to punish yourself for it. Many people tend to stress out when this slipup happens, and then they go forward and binge-eat, which just makes it worse. Let go of the small stuff and focus on the big picture. Start saying no to food even if it is offered to you when you know you shouldn't be eating it. This simple no will help you avoid the stress of feeling guilty and the retaliation of overeating later.

Slowly but surely you will learn to deal with the triggers that make you eat emotionally. You need to address them if you want to solve the problem. Think about why you turn to food when a particular situation comes up and plan out how you will react and deal with it when it happens again. This will help you to turn away from emotional eating when you are stressed, lonely, or just feeling low about your body image.

Repeat the Process for Any Trigger

The steps given above might help you through a few triggers initially, but you have to learn to apply them for all sorts of triggers in the future. There are different levels of emotional dependency on food. Some people may be triggered by only a few factors while others have a variety of things that push them toward emotional eating. Emotional eating that has developed for years will take a bit of time to deal with. You don't have to stress about solving your problems all at once. Work through it slowly and step by step. This will help you be more thorough and process it better. Deal with one trigger at a time and appreciate the progress you make.

As you identify and deal with all your triggers, you will soon see that you no longer depend on emotional eating to deal with emotions or situations. This is when you will know that you are free from emotional eating and have a healthier relationship with food. Take notice of when a trigger occurs and see how you react to it. If you don't think about food or turn to eating, then you have definitely resolved it. Initially, you might get the urge to eat, but over time you will learn how to control yourself. After a while, this trigger will not be a trigger anymore. Give yourself some self-appreciation for all the progress you make.

The process does not end here. Emotional eating has many aspects that you need to deal with. It can take anywhere from months to years to completely get rid of the problem. You have to slowly take steps to build a healthier relationship with food and become independent of it emotionally. All the information in this book is essential to help you understand and deal with it.

Treatments for Emotional Eating

In order to overcome emotional eating, there are many things you need to deal with. You have to learn to establish a healthier relationship with food and manage stress in a better way. You need to recognize your triggers and develop appropriate responses for them. There are many healthier ways to deal with stress. Start engaging in some regular exercise that will reduce the production of stress hormones. Physical activity helps to decrease symptoms of anxiety and depression and even improves sleep cycles. All this will, in turn, reduce the tendency to stress-eat.

One of the easiest and most creative ways to start with your treatment is creating a vision board. A vision board helps you to envision a much brighter future and stay motivated. It is a way to express yourself and your emotions creatively. It is actually very simple to create a vision board that aids in your recovery. Take a piece cardboard or plain poster of any size you want and a lot of craft supplies. Find inspiration from pictures, music and/or sentences that motivate you. Cut these out or write them in big letters on your board. Envision the things that you aim for in your future like traveling or a big family. Don't look at pictures of models with photo-shopped bodies. Your aim is to turn your focus towards more positive goals. You don't have to worry about what form the board takes. Be creative and let it flow. Once you are done, hang the board in a place that is in your line of vision. You should be able to see it as often as possible. You can always add things or make changes. Aim to fulfill some of the goals that you write on your board and you will see progress. A vision board can just be a positive art that you create for yourself.

One of the best ways to manage stress and emotional eating is meditation and similar relaxation techniques. Try to start meditating once or twice a day for at least ten minutes each time. Engaging in these short sessions will have a beneficial effect on your mind and body. You will much calmer and more focused, and your blood pressure and heart rate will also be regulated.

One of the worst ways to deal with stress is resorting to drugs and alcohol. These actually heighten your response to stress and are detrimental to your body. Just like food, these substances will alter your state of mind only temporarily and will not let you effectively cope with the situation. Staying away from drugs and limiting alcohol intake will be a very positive change.

Start making some positive lifestyle changes. Instead of letting yourself get overwhelmed with work, take breaks. Don't take on more than you can handle. Monetary success should not come at the cost of mental and physical well-being. Work issues are one of the common triggers of emotional eating. Take some days off when you can't handle the pressure. More importantly, learn to balance things in a way that you can handle properly.

Family therapy is another element that has proven to be helpful in the treatment of eating disorders. Family plays an important role in your life and getting them involved in your therapy can play an important role. Therapy will help you and your family learn how to communicate better, manage conflicts, overcome negative emotions during this period, etc. It also helps the patient understand what impact their illness had on the family and others around them. It helps the family to understand what the person is suffering from and that the illness does not define them. Lack of information about eating disorders causes a lot of conflict in many families. Even during the process of recovery, families can find it hard to see the person suffering. Therapy helps every family member, as well as the individual themselves come to terms with all the emotions and experiences involved when someone suffers from an eating disorder.

If stress is a major concern for you, try some stress management counseling. There are many therapists who can help you out with this and many group therapy sessions held for people just like you. Listening to their stories and gaining guidance might help you out. These kinds of sessions have proven to be beneficial for people with many different problems. One of the most effective treatments for this has been cognitive behavioral therapy. Therapists use this approach to change the patient's attitude toward certain situations. There are three techniques involved in this therapy.

The first is the didactic component, which helps the patient set some positive expectations from the therapy. This helps to improve their cooperation with the therapy as they work to fulfill those expectations. The second phase is the cognitive component where they help in identifying the thoughts that influence the person's behavior. This is particularly focused on anything that makes the person more susceptible to emotional eating. The cognitive component often involves teaching the person mindful eating to improve their relationship with food and help them become more aware of their emotions. The third component is the behavioral one. This phase allows the therapist to use techniques to modify a person's behavior in order to stop emotional eating. It teaches them more effective ways to deal with the triggers that initially caused them to turn toward emotional eating. Cognitive behavioral therapy has gained a lot of positive feedback from people suffering from emotional eating.

You can also go to self-help group sessions like Overeaters Anonymous, which allow you to meet random people with the same problems. This kind of group is a very healthy resource that will help you recognize and cope with all your triggers in a better way. You can use the sessions to gain support and guidance on how you should deal with your stress and overeating. There are many nutritionists and therapists that can help you on your journey to a healthier life. All you need to do is reach out.

Chapter 6: Organizations and Support Groups

Like we mentioned above, it can be extremely helpful to join support groups or forums that specifically deal with eating disorders. Here you can get guidance from professionals and meet other people who have suffered similar issues. Learning from their experience will help you in your journey and boost your morale. There are numerous such groups all over and you can definitely find some in your area. We have mentioned some of that you might find useful.

- Eating Disorders Anonymous

- ANAD Eating Disorder Support Group

- Compulsive Eaters Anonymous

- Eating Disorders Resource Centre

- Friends and Family Support Group

- Hope- Eating Disorder Support Group

- Overeaters Anonymous Meeting

- Rosewood support groups

- "Lift the Shame" Online Support Group

- Alsana Eating Recovery Family Online Support Group

- Milestones in Recovery Online Support Group

- The National Association For Males with Eating

Disorders

- Eating Disorders Anonymous Online Meeting

- Healing Cove

There are hundreds of more places near you where you can find support for yourself and your family while battling this illness. Take the initiative to find one that suits your needs. Support groups will definitely aid in your recovery.

Chapter 7: Stress Management

Stress is one of the evils that most of us face in our daily lives. There are two types of stress that we experience—one is acute stress, and the other is chronic stress. Normal stress is what our body is conditioned to deal with. When there is a threat, our body becomes alert and reacts to it. There is a surge of hormones that allows us to take immediate action to enable self-preservation. This fight-or-flight response is acute stress. The body returns to its normal state when this stress passes.

Chronic stress is when the body stays in this stressful state for a long time, and this is a problem. Acute stress is a normal bodily response that is beneficial for us, but chronic stress only causes problems. Stress increases hormones that cause hunger and lead to increased cravings. This stress also reduces the hormones that tell you when you have eaten enough. This is why you feel very hungry and eat more than you need to when you're stressed. Ultimately all the overeating will cause weight gain and inflammation and lead to diseases. Understanding the biological implication of stress is important if you want to know how it affects your body.

Every time you are stressed out or suffering from chronic stress, you will have a tendency to reach for comfort foods. These foods provide the instant gratification you're accustomed to. The situations causing the stress in your life don't grant this gratification, so you turn to food. Instead of reaching for nutritious, healthy food that will benefit our body, we reach for something that will give us a quick but temporary boost. In these stressful situations, we don't remember that the junk food that gives us momentary pleasure will end up being another reason to feel guilty and stressed. This is why you need to combat this kind of habit and learn to deal with stress in a healthier way.

You need to realize and accept that you are the priority in your life. This does not mean that you are selfish but that you give yourself some much-deserved self-love and appreciation, which will in turn reduce your stress levels. Stress often makes us sacrifice our own well-being, and we do more for others than ourselves. When there is too much pressure at work, we stress out over it but somehow complete it to satisfy our peers. Instead, you should be taking it slow and pacing your work to suit you. Trying to keep up with someone else's pace will do nothing but add stress to your life. Make your needs your priority. This is not the same as slacking off at work. It just means that you don't take on more work than you can physically or mentally handle.

Start setting aside some time every day to listen to your body and stay free from any distractions. Think of your emotions and how you have been feeling lately. Use this time to re-commit yourself to your health goals. Stop bottling up your emotions and ignoring your inner voice. Don't clamp down on what you are feeling. It will just affect your mental health and your relationships with others as well. This kind of emotional suppression triggers unhealthy emotional eating. Let yourself experience all you are feeling, and be compassionate toward yourself. Slowly you will become comfortable with dealing with uncomfortable emotions instead of suppressing them with food.

Stop skipping meals no matter how busy you are. Even if you have a huge workload, you need to prioritize your health. Even though stress causes you to binge on junk food, it might make you forget about your proper meals. Skipping meals will just drop the energy levels in your body that you need to work optimally.

If you go too long without eating, you are more prone to a sudden onset of hunger where you will overeat unhealthy foods. Instead, prioritize mealtimes and eat healthy, nutritious food that you won't feel guilty about later. Timely meals will help avoid cravings to a large extent. When you don't eat for a long time, your body goes into stress mode. When you eat after that period, your body stores the food differently compared to a healthy meal. A lot of the food will go into fat storage to prepare for the next time that you skip your meals. This means that you will be gaining weight even though you skip meals. So don't try to lose weight by doing this.

If you want to eat healthier, make a healthy meal schedule. Plan three meals at the right times for breakfast, lunch, and dinner. Don't let the gap between these meals be too long. and keep a few healthy snacks at hand in case you feel hungry in between. Always make sure to eat a healthy breakfast. This will help to stabilize the blood sugar levels in your body. Better eating habits will increase your productivity and also balance stress levels.

Choose the right kinds of food to include in your diet. Junk food can make stressful conditions worse. They are devoid of any actual nutrition and filled with fats and sugars that are bad for your body. Nutrient-rich foods are more beneficial because they support the health of the body in every way and regulate the stress response as well. Proper food can improve immunity, reduce the risk of diseases, increase energy levels, and just generally improve performance.

Meditation is one of the keys to dealing with stress. Although the practice has existed for centuries, people all over the world have started implementing it in recent years. Some of the most successful people in the world have said that meditation has benefited them in more ways than one. Meditation helps in focusing on the present and slowing down the pace of your mind. You learn to feel what is going on inside your body without being distracted by the outside environment.

Meditation has shown to reduce cortisol levels to a large extent. We already know that cortisol is mainly linked to stress in our body, so reducing it is ideal. Meditation helps you to feel less stressed and improve your daily habits in a healthier way. You will start eating better, feeling better, and doing much better in all your tasks. Reducing stress is crucial in dealing with emotional eating, and meditation helps a lot. You might not be confident about its effectiveness, but once you try it for a while, you will see a difference. Start by setting aside some time every day to meditate. Fifteen minutes of meditation in the morning is ideal to begin your day with.

Download a meditation app or some meditation music to help guide you. Find a corner in the house that is free of distractions. You could even try to practice it in an open space like the park or your roof. The fresh air will make the experience even better. Make this meditation practice a part of your daily life just like you brush your teeth every morning. You won't see any miraculous change in a day or two, but you will feel the difference soon enough.

Tips for Reducing Stress:

- Learn to accept that not everything is under your control.

- Practice relaxation techniques like meditation, tai chi, or yoga to deal with stress.

- Eat a balanced diet.

- Manage your time more efficiently so that you're not overloaded with work and pressure.

- Make time for things you enjoy like hobbies or traveling.

- Say no to anything that does not benefit you and will impact your mental and physical health. You don't have to please others all the time.

- Exercise regularly to combat stress hormones.

- Stop being aggressive and be more assertive in all that you do and feel.

- Set a proper sleep cycle that allows you to get enough rest every day.

- Don't resort to drugs, alcohol, or even junk food to combat stressful situations.

- Set limits for everything and don't overdo it.

- Ask for support from friends and family or a stress management support group.

- Use tools that will help you manage your work, meals, and daily habits in an easier way. Setting up a plan on your calendar will help you allocate appropriate time for everything. Don't try to multitask and strain yourself.

Reducing Stress with your Diet:

There are many ways to use food to reduce stress levels in your body. Instead of eating to suppress stress, you can add some things to your diet that help improve the condition.

- Try a hot cup of tea to calm yourself. Herbs like lavender or chamomile add extra ingredients to a warm cup of tea that can be very soothing for your mind. These have shown to have a very relaxing effect just from their aroma.

- Instead of eating too many cookies and calorific chocolates, eat some dark chocolate. Dark chocolate is rich in antioxidants and will help reduce the stress hormone levels in the body. It's still chocolate, so you feel like you're indulging yourself, but you are also benefiting from it. As long as you don't overindulge in it, it can have a positive impact on you.

- Opt for healthy carbohydrates in your diet; don't cut them all off just to lose weight. Research has shown that carbohydrates increase serotonin levels. Serotonin is a hormone that reduces stress and improves your mood. To be more weight-conscious, try to add healthy options like sweet potatoes instead of white potatoes.

- The omega-3 fatty acids in fatty fish are a great addition to your diet because they are good for cardiovascular health. These fatty acids are known to improve nerve cell communication and help alleviate depression. Fatty fish are also quite delicious, so there's no reason not to indulge.

- Try having some warm milk before you go to bed. It's

an age-old practice said to reduce stress and calm you down for a good night's sleep. It will help to relax your muscles and mind at the same time.

- Nuts are a great snack that will help to reduce stress as well. They're high in calories, so a handful a day is enough.

- Add vitamin C to your diet in the recommended daily quantity. Many studies have shown vitamin C to lower stress levels in the body by reducing cortisol levels. Fruits like oranges and strawberries are a great way to add this to your diet.

Stress is a problem that is overlooked by most people until it's too late. It's actually one of the major contributors to many health issues in this fast-paced day and age. It increases the risk for heart conditions and diseases like diabetes. It makes you eat more to suppress emotions and disrupts your healthy eating cycle. Stress also causes sleep cycle disruption and is often a cause for insomnia even in younger people. You need to pay attention to the symptoms and causes of any stress in your life. The main focus of this book with regards to stress is the emotional eating caused by it. Stress is one of the major trigger factors that makes you turn toward emotional eating to feel better; however, the food won't make the cause of stress or the stress itself go away. It will remain in your mind and build up until you resolve it. This is why this book places so much emphasis on how you should manage stress in your life.

Chapter 8: Mindful Eating

To curb emotional eating, you need to establish a much healthier relationship with food. Emotional eaters experience sudden and uncontrollable urges to eat comfort food when they are triggered. Mindful eating is a practice that will help you become more aware of how, what, and when you eat. This practice will help you control your reaction to triggers and food cravings.

The tension builds in a way that makes you feel the need to satisfy the sudden hunger pangs immediately; however, this is not actual physical hunger but just emotional hunger. It's a temporary way to fill some sort of mental void with food. You might have tried to resist these urges and failed in the past. This could possibly make you feel like you don't have enough willpower to deal with the issue, but honestly, you do.

A lot of research has shown that distraction during a meal does not allow a person to enjoy or appreciate their food. This mindless eating is actually linked to stress, anxiety, and overeating issues in people. If you want to know whether you are a mindful or mindless eater, think about the last meal you ate. Do you remember how it tasted, smelled, or felt in your mouth? Like most people, you probably don't. Mindful eating will help you to be more in touch with the experience of eating. Mindfulness while eating will enhance your eating experience, bringing it to a much higher level even for the simplest foods that you consume every day. You will learn to pause and focus on what you are about to eat every time. This allows you to get rid of the habit of mindless emotional eating.

Emotional eating is a way of mindlessly and automatically reaching for food when you have to deal with any negative emotions or stress. The ice cream is polished off before you realize it. You reach out and start eating the cookies till the jar is empty. This mindless reaction is a major problem. Give yourself the opportunity to make a decision about actually eating the food instead of just reaching for it. When you get a craving, stop for a moment and think about it. Are you really hungry? Should you eat that food?

Start off by waiting a minute every time a craving hits you. Don't think about overcoming the craving and ignoring the urge to eat. Just allow yourself to wait a minute or two before you touch the food. Tell yourself that you just have to wait a few minutes before you eat. During this waiting period, ask yourself some questions. Think about how you're feeling at the time. Take note of your emotions right then. It's okay if you decide to go ahead and eat after this, but these few moments allow you to understand what emotions pushed you to eat. You can use this to your benefit the next time.

Your emotional eating does not stem from powerlessness over food. The problem is not with food but with emotions and situations. When you feel like you can't or don't want to deal with certain emotions, you turn toward food to avoid them. Eating helps you suppress the stress and push it to the back of your mind.

Emotions can be scary, and you may feel uncomfortable dealing with them. Many people are unwilling to open up to their emotions because they fear a lack of power when it's all let loose, but if you're really honest and give yourself the chance to deal with emotions when they arise, you will see that it is better than suppressing or obsessing over them for a long time.

Give yourself time and allow yourself to feel the emotions as they come. Even if it is immense grief over the loss of a loved one, it's better to experience it in that moment. You might think otherwise, but even the most powerful of emotions tend to subside quite quickly. Suppressing such emotions just allows them to build up over time until they may come out in an emotional breakdown. Dealing with your emotions as soon as they occur means that they lose control over you after a while. In order to do this, you need to learn to be more mindful of each moment. Mindfulness encourages you to bring yourself to the present and not remain preoccupied with the past.

One of the most beneficial aspects of mindfulness is mindful eating. This practice can be helpful for emotional eaters as they learn how to enjoy their meals more but with moderation. It teaches them how to practice restraint and improve eating habits.

Principles of Mindful Eating

- Mindful eating helps to increase awareness about the positive and nurturing aspect of food.

- It allows you to use all your senses in choosing what you want to eat so that it's satisfying to your mind and body.

- Mindful eating also helps you acknowledge what foods you like or dislike without any judgment.

- It helps you differentiate real hunger from emotional eating and allows you to make the right decisions about when you should eat.

- It allows the individual to accept that each person's

eating experiences are unique.

- It makes you aware of how you can make choices that will support your mental and physical well-being.

- With practice, it allows you to free yourself from habitual patterns that are destructive and don't benefit you in any way.

- It also allows you to become more aware of your internal and external environment and encompass both.

The following points will help you in eating with more mindfulness as you combat your emotional eating.

Tips for mindful eating:

- Start by reflecting on your emotions before you begin a meal. Think about how you're feeling and all the emotions rushing through your mind. Differentiate between physical hunger and cravings caused by stress or boredom. Then make the choice to eat or not to eat accordingly. It's up to you to eat even if you're not really hungry, but the choice needs to be made consciously and not out of habit.

- Don't eat when you are doing something else or going somewhere. Be seated for every meal. Multitasking during meals does not allow you to appreciate your food. Eating on the go also does not allow you to keep track of your food as you should.

- Don't eat mindlessly while watching TV or playing with

your phone. You are distracted while doing these and don't pay attention to what or how much you eat. This is one of the easiest ways to consume too many snacks that lead to weight gain.

- Be mindful about portions for meals as well as snacks. Don't eat right out of a box. You can't keep track of the food or even appreciate what you're eating. Portions served on plates or bowls is a better way to eat.

- Control your portion sizes. Instead of the larger plates and bowls, use the smaller ones. It's very easy to fill up a big plate with too much food. A smaller plate will help you take only as much as you need. If you still feel hungry, you can serve yourself another portion. Just because you go to an all-you-can-eat buffet does not mean you have to eat a lot. Appreciate the variety of options there instead of the amount you can stuff into your body. Use smaller plates to eat more of what you really like.

- Chewing your food is essential for proper digestion, and it helps you become more aware of how many bites you take. Try chewing each bit of food at least ten times to start with. Allow yourself time to enjoy the flavor of the food and don't just push it down your throat in an attempt to eat as much as possible. As opposed to fast eating, taking your time to eat usually helps to prevent overeating. Your body needs time to send the message that it's full. Eating quickly does not allow this to happen appropriately.

- You don't have to finish all the food on your plate every time. This is something we were all taught while growing up, but it is not compulsory. The ideal would be to serve yourself only as much as you really need or will eat, and if there is too much on your plate and you feel full at a certain point, then just stop eating. Leaving a few bites on your plate won't feed the poor, but it will help you exercise more control over your eating habits. You can always give the leftovers to your dog to enjoy.

- Eat quietly and without any distractions once in a while. This allows you to pay more attention to the texture, flavor, and smell of what is in your mouth. Dinner conversations can be fun, but they don't allow you to pay due attention to your food at times.

- Practice gratitude. Take a few moments before every meal to be grateful for all the effort it took to bring the meal on your plate. Gratitude toward food is a very positive and mindful attitude.

Mindfulness has many benefits in every aspect of your life. With regard to food, you learn how to eat much better and develop a healthy relationship with food. Emotional eating is mindless and the exact opposite of mindful eating. As you embrace the present, you still start appreciating the food, company, and everything in your life in a more positive manner.

Alternatives to Emotional Eating

You need to learn to manage your emotions in a different way if you want to stop eating. Emotional eating won't solve anything. It will only add to all your problems. It's not just about controlling your diet because diets fail all the time. A healthy and nutritious diet is important, but you also have to find a way to deal with the emotions associated with your eating habits.

For instance, if you feel depressed, then call someone who is always supportive and kind to you. Play with your pets if you don't want to talk to another person. If you don't already have a dog, we highly recommend one. Dogs have been shown to help many people deal with stress and live a more positive life. Otherwise just turn to your family or your closest friends who love you. Don't try to channel all the negativity inside yourself.

If you feel anxious about something, don't reach for food or sit around thinking about it. Do some kind of physical activity like dancing. You can go for a walk in the park as well. This will help relieve your stress and make you feel better.

Treat yourself to a hot bath with some essential oils when you feel very tired. Drink some hot tea or light some scented candles. Do anything that will make you feel a little better.

When you're bored, don't turn toward mindless eating. Read a book or watch a funny show. Go for a ride or play a sport you enjoy. Don't allow yourself to get bored and eat when you have nothing to do.

All of these are just some simple alternatives to emotional eating when you're faced with common triggers. You might not conquer your habits in a day or two, but you will do much better soon enough. Be patient with yourself and stop eating to deal with your feelings. There are much better ways to help yourself feel better.

Conclusion

Now that you have come to the end of the book, I would first like to thank you for reading. All the information and research for this book was taken from various sources to help you understand emotional eating and the reasons behind it so that you can stop eating and start living a healthier life.

Most people don't even realize the reasons behind all the overeating or stress-eating that leads to other problems in their life. Stress is one of the main problems that you have to learn to deal with in a healthier way. Once you realize that you have a problem and an unhealthy emotional dependency on food, you need to work to start changing this.

Start becoming more conscious of all the triggers that make you turn toward food for comfort. Question why you react this way and change it. Don't shy away from problems and emotions. Find a healthier way to channel your emotions and don't suppress them with food. The problems that make you stress-eat need to be resolved if you don't want them to recur. Ignoring them will not make them go away. When you deal with the problems at hand, they don't pile up, and you will feel much more relieved than you possibly could with some food.

Aim for long-term happiness and not temporary solutions. If you don't control the overeating in time, you will gain more weight than your body can handle. This will only add to all the problems you already face. Learning to deal with emotional eating will help you in improving many other aspects in your life. You will learn how to manage stress better, eat better, and become more mindful of your actions. You will start facing problems and learn how to resolve them properly. You won't eat unnecessary amounts food and instead will eat only when you're really hungry. You will start becoming more conscious of all that you do.

All in all, you will be on the path to a genuinely happy life. All these changes will improve your mental health, physical health, and even the appearance of your body. So why not make the effort to implement all these positive changes in your life if all you have to do is stop eating? If you find this book helpful in your journey, go ahead and recommend or gift it to others who could benefit from it as well, please feel free to leave a review on amazon.com.

References

National Eating Disorders Association. (2018). Retrieved from https://www.nationaleatingdisorders.org/

Made in the USA
Lexington, KY
26 March 2019